MW01267735

Reading Essentials® in Science

EARTH EXPLORATIONS II

Changing Shorelines

TRACI STECKEL PEDERSEN

PERFECTION LEARNING®

Editorial Director: Susan C. Thies
Editor: Mary L. Bush
Design Director: Randy Messer
Book Design: Brian Shearer, Robin Elwick, Tobi Cunningham
Cover Design: Michael A. Aspengren

A special thanks to the following for his scientific review of the book:
Kristin Mandsager, Instructor of Physics and Astronomy,
Garden City Community College

Image Credits:
©George H. H. Huey/CORBIS: cover; ©Paul A. Souders/Corbis: pp. 5, 8 (bottom); ©Marc Serota/Reuters/
Corbis: p. 23 (top); ©Yann Arthus-Bertrand/Corbis: p. 28; ©Gary Bell/Australian Picture Library/CORBIS:
p. 29; ©Victor Ruiz/Reuters/Corbis: p. 34

photos.com: pp. 1, 3, 4, 6 (bottom), 7 (top), 8 (top), 9 (top), 10, 11, 12 (top), 13, 14 (top), 16,
17, 18, 19, 20, 21 (bottom), 22, 26 (top), 31 (top), 32, 33, 36, 37, 39, 40; istockphoto.com:
back cover, pp. 15 (bottom), 21 (top), 23 (bottom), 24 (top), 25, 27 (bottom), 30, 31 (bottom), 35;
Corel: p. 24 (bottom); Map Resources: p. 26 (bottom); PLC: pp. 6 (top), 7 (bottom), 9 (bottom),
12 (bottom), 14 (bottom), 15 (top), 27 (top)

For information, contact
Perfection Learning® Corporation
1000 North Second Avenue, P.O. Box 500
Logan, Iowa 51546-0500.
Phone: 1-800-831-4190
Fax: 1-800-543-2745
perfectionlearning.com

1 2 3 4 5 6 PP 12 11 10 09 08 07

PB ISBN 0-7891-7036-1
RLB ISBN 0-7569-6656-6

Table of Contents

Standing on the Shore

You and your friends are headed to the beach for the day. Your plans include a game of sand volleyball, splashing around in the water, and lying on a towel soaking up the sun. While you're lying there enjoying the sound of the waves splashing up onto the shore, do you ever stop to think about how the beach was formed or how it changes from day to day or year to year? Do you ever consider what you could do to ensure that the beach remains safe and healthy for years to come?

Millions of people live or vacation near shorelines. A shoreline is the area where a body of water meets land. The land near the shoreline is called a *coast*, *shore*, or *beach*.

Every shoreline is unique. The temperature and movement of the water differ. The composition of the land varies. Even the plant and animal life is different from shore to shore.

Whether it's a soft, sandy beach or a rugged, rocky coast, a shoreline is always changing. Weather, water, geography, and human activity cause these changes. Some of the changes are positive. Others are not. Regardless, one thing is for sure—a beach is never exactly the same two days in a row.

The Formation of Shorelines

Shorelines can be classified according to how they were formed. There are two basic types of shorelines—primary and secondary. Primary shorelines can be further categorized as emergent or submergent.

Primary Shorelines

Primary coasts are formed by processes that occur on land. The **erosion** and **deposition** of **sediment** by wind, rain, rivers, or glaciers can shape shorelines. Lava that spews from volcanoes can cool and harden into new shoreline. When pieces of the Earth's crust called **tectonic plates** shift during an earthquake, new shorelines may emerge.

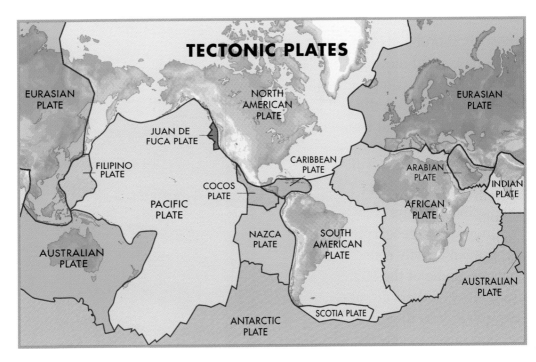

TECTONIC PLATES

Deltas and lava coasts are examples of primary shorelines. A delta arises when a river deposits sediment before draining into an ocean. A lava coast is formed when lava flows from a volcano and hardens at the edge of an ocean.

Lava coast

Delta Details

A delta is a triangular area of land where a river meets an ocean. As a river approaches an ocean, it "dumps" much of the sediment it's picked up right before it flows into the ocean. This sediment accumulates in thick layers, creating land with nutrient-rich soil. Often this land is used for farming, but it has also been used for building cities. The city of New Orleans in Louisiana, for example, sits on the Mississippi River Delta.

River delta

Primary shorelines are either emergent or submergent. Emergent shorelines are a result of tectonic activity or post-glacial rebound. When tectonic plates shift, land may be pushed upward, forming a shoreline along an ocean. Large masses of ice known as glaciers press down on the land they cover. As these glaciers melt, the land "rebounds" by rising upward. This is called *post-glacial rebound*. Some of this rising land becomes shoreline.

Rising sea levels reveal submergent shorelines. These shorelines are shaped by melting glaciers that cause sea levels to rise. Old shorelines sink beneath the rising water and new ones evolve.

Post-Glacial Rebound

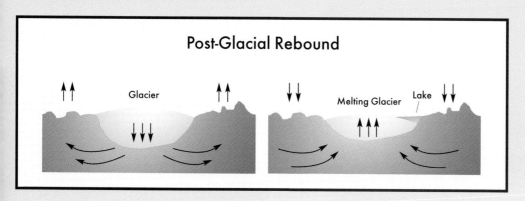

Glacier

Melting Glacier   Lake

Secondary Shorelines

Secondary shorelines are formed by processes that occur in the water. **Wave** erosion, **current** deposition, and marine animals are

Great Barrier Reef

responsible for creating secondary shorelines. When ocean water moves onto land, it drops off sediment. As it recedes, it picks up sediment from the land and carries it back out to sea. This "exchange" of sediment builds up and washes away shorelines on a continual basis. Moving water also wears away rock, carving out shorelines. Marine animals called *coral polyps* form reefs, which can rise above the surface, creating a shoreline. Rocky cliffs, marshes, **barrier islands**, and coral reefs are examples of secondary shorelines.

Zoning In on
Shorelines

2

$\mathbf{W}$alking along a shore can be a very different experience depending on *where* you walk. If you walk along the water's edge, you can enjoy the refreshing feel of the waves lapping over your feet. Higher up on shore, the sand may be wet and squishy beneath your feet, but otherwise you remain dry. At the back of the beach, walking in bare feet may be uncomfortable because the sand there is typically hot and dry. Water from the ocean rarely reaches this area of the beach.

Shore Zones

The land along a shoreline can be divided into zones. Each zone has different characteristics.

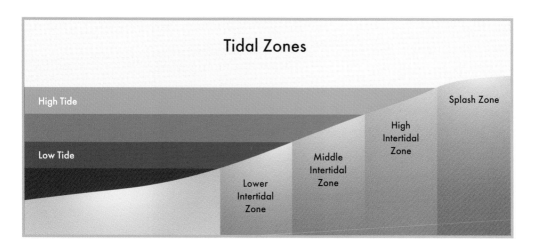

Tidal Zones

High Tide

Low Tide

Lower Intertidal Zone

Middle Intertidal Zone

High Intertidal Zone

Splash Zone

Splash Zone

The highest zone is the splash, or spray, zone. This area is beyond the reach of high **tides**. It is only occasionally "splashed" or submerged during intense storms. Plants and animals that can tolerate a salty environment and prolonged exposure to air can live in this zone.

Intertidal Zones

The remaining zones are affected by the tides. Tides are the regular rising and falling of ocean water due mainly to the gravitational pull of the Moon. Different locations on a beach are covered by varying amounts of water when the tide comes in. This determines if a location is in the high, middle, or lower intertidal zone.

The high intertidal zone is dry most of the time. It is covered with water only during very high tides. Plants and animals in this zone need to be able to survive long periods without water. They must also be able to withstand strong gushes of water when the tide does reach them.

If you've ever laid out your beach towel on a dry spot only to find it dripping wet in a few hours, you're in the middle intertidal zone. This is the area of the shore that's dry at low tide but covered with water during high tide. Because of the regular flooding with water, temperatures are less extreme than in zones farther back on the beach. The moisture and milder temperatures make this zone more hospitable for a variety of animals. Many of these animals are successful because they have adaptations for "staying put" when the tide rushes in and out.

The lower intertidal zone is the wettest area on the shore. This zone stays wet most of the time, except at extremely low tides. The lower intertidal zone experiences less change than other zones. There's a consistent source of water, exposure to sunlight for **photosynthesis**, and milder temperatures. These conditions make this zone ideal for numerous species of aquatic organisms.

Sea anemones thrive in middle and lower intertidal zones because they have an adhesive disk at their base that holds them in place when the tide comes in or goes out.

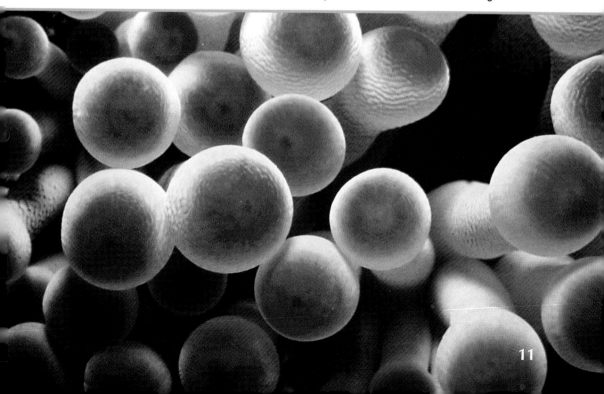

Tide Talk

What causes the tides that affect life along a shoreline? As the Earth rotates, different sides of the Earth face the Moon. The Moon's force of gravity is stronger on the side of the Earth that directly faces the Moon. This makes the ocean water "bulge" toward the Moon, causing water levels on that side of the Earth to rise. On the opposite side of the Earth, the Moon's force of attraction is weaker, so the water bulges away from the Moon, pulling water up onto the land. These periods of high water are known as high tides. As the Earth rotates, the water returns to the ocean, resulting in low tides. High and low tides alternately return to any given spot every 12 hours and 25 minutes. When they do, they change the dynamics of a shoreline.

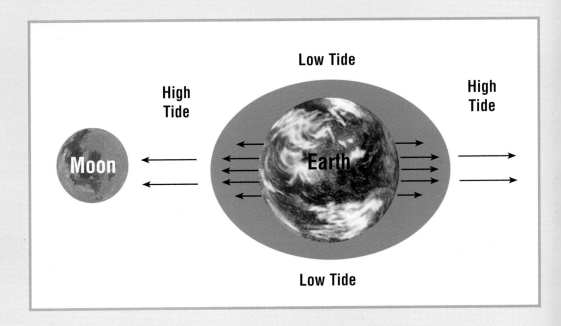

3

Sandy Shores

When most people think of the beach, they think of sand. Sandy shores are indeed covered with sand. What is sand? Sand is tiny bits of rock, shells, and animal skeletons.

The sand on a particular beach is generally characterized by the type of minerals found in the rocks nearby. These rocks are eroded by wind and water to form finely ground sand consisting of mineral particles. Depending on the minerals, a beach may be covered with sand that's tan, pink, white, black, purple, or a mixture of colors. Quartz and feldspar make up much of the world's sandy beaches. These minerals are found in rock such as granite and sandstone and come in a variety of colors such as white, tan, and pink. Black sand comes from eroded lava rock or rocks containing the mineral iron.

Moving and Changing

Sandy beaches are shaped by wind and water action. Waves and currents are constantly moving sand and changing the landscape of a sandy beach.

Waves are caused by the transfer of energy from the wind. As wind blows across the surface of the water, it pushes on the water, creating friction. This friction makes ripples in the water as energy is transferred from the wind to the water. The strength and duration of the wind determine the size and force of the waves.

Waves approach a beach at an angle. As the waves recede to the ocean, however, they reorganize into a straight line, so they don't deposit sand at the same spot where they arrived onshore. Instead, the movement of the waves and the deposition of sand follow a zigzag pattern along the shoreline. This process is known as **beach drift**.

Beach drift

Direction of wa

As waves push toward a shoreline, a **longshore current** moves alongside it. A current is a "river" of water traveling within an ocean. A longshore current is a current running parallel to a shoreline. Sediment that's "kicked up" by approaching waves is carried along by the longshore current and is eventually deposited along the shoreline. When a large amount of sediment is deposited quickly, a longshore current may build a long ridge of sand known as a **sandbar**.

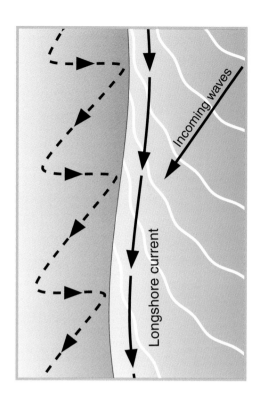

Fast and Furious Erosion

Daily wind and water action brings consistent change to sandy beaches. But sometimes intense storms can change the look of a beach overnight. Many coasts are exposed to hurricanes. These violent storms bring fierce winds, pounding rains, and walls of water that can wash away sand at a tremendous rate. It can take years for a beach to recover from the destructive force of a hurricane.

Winter beach

Seasonal Changes

If you were to visit the same sandy beach in the summer and in the winter, you would notice big changes. Large waves tend to wash sand away, stripping a beach. Smaller waves tend to deposit sand on a beach, building it up. In the winter, long periods of large waves remove much of the sand from a beach. An early spring beach may be almost bare. In the summer, calmer waves replace much of the lost sand, restoring the beach to its original sandy state.

Summer beach

Sand Dunes

Farther up the beach, away from the water, wind erosion can change the shape of a beach. As sea breezes and strong winds blow over the beach, sand is pushed backward and stacks up at the back of the beach. These piles of sand are called **sand dunes**. Wind and waves coming from the ocean slowly push sand dunes backward on a beach.

A beach may have more than one row of dunes. The dunes closest to the ocean are called *primary dunes*, while the dunes behind them are called *secondary dunes*. The primary dunes form a barrier against ocean flooding. The secondary dunes provide a place for plant growth that helps stabilize the dunes. The dry sand in dunes isn't a good place for most plants to grow, but some grasses, such as marram grass and sea oats, thrive in the sandy soil. The roots of the grasses help hold the sand in place. Without the grass, strong winds would blow the dunes away. This would leave the land beyond the beach open to flooding.

Damaging the Dunes

Wind erosion isn't the only cause of changes to sand dunes. Human actions also contribute to the erosion and destruction of dunes. Dunes are often disturbed by pedestrians, off-road vehicles, and construction work. People and vehicles trample plants as they travel across dunes. Construction workers level dunes for buildings and roads. The disappearance of sand and vegetation not only harms the dunes directly affected, but it also opens nearby dunes to further wind erosion.

4

Rocky Shores

While you can't build sand castles on a rocky shore, you can skip rocks, walk on huge boulders, and watch birds that nest in the cliffs. Rocky coasts are secondary coasts formed by wave erosion and deposition. The rocks along the shoreline vary from shore to shore. Some rocky shores feature tall cliffs that may have little or no beach below them. Others are beaches lined with boulders, pebbles, or gravel deposited by the ocean.

Rocky shores form where most of the sediment has not been worn down into tiny particles of sand. Sand may be present among the sediment on a rocky shore, but it is more likely to stay in the water while larger, heavier sediment settles on the beach. Over time, a layer of pebbles accumulates. Steep shores tend to hold less sediment because the tall slopes send incoming sediment back out to sea. Gently sloping shores "catch" more sediment.

Tide Pools

Tide pools are often found in rocky intertidal zones. A tide pool is an area of water trapped between large rocks when high tidewaters flow onto a shore. Tide pools are also called *rock pools*. These pools are home to many organisms on a rocky shore.

Although a "pool" sounds like a great place to call home, a tide pool is actually a tough place to live. The environment in a tide pool changes daily with the tides. When the tide comes in, water fills the pool. When the tide goes out, all or most of the water in the pool goes with it. Tide pool animals must have adaptations for staying put when the tide comes in and staying cool and hydrated when the tide goes out.

The deepest tide pools, which are closest to the ocean, host the most sea life because they generally retain some water when the tide goes out. Shallower tide pools farther up the shore are inhabited by only the toughest of the tide pool residents.

Carving Out Changes: Sea Caves, Capes, Arches, and Sea Stacks

Powerful waves are capable of carving sea caves along rocky coasts. Sea caves often begin as cracks in weak spots on a cliff. These weak areas may be **faults** where tectonic plate movement caused breaks in the rock or places where weaker rock is imbedded in stronger rock. Crashing waves make their way into cracks in a cliff and then wear away at the opening until a cave is formed.

The inside of a sea cave may be wet or dry, depending on the tides and wave action. A variety of animals make their homes inside sea caves, including many of the same creatures that live in tide pools.

Sea cave in the Iles de la Madeleine, Québec

Cape Point, South Africa

A **cape** is a narrow piece of land that extends from a rocky coast. It is easily eroded because it is "attacked" by waves on three sides. This erosion may lead to the formation of a sea cave, arch, or sea stack.

When both sides of a cape are eroded to form a narrow ridge and the rock beneath is hollowed out, an arch is created. An arch resembles a bridge. Sometimes the top of an arch collapses, leaving just a tall stack of rock behind. This new rocky landform is called a *sea stack*.

Arch along the coast of Brittany, France

5

Soggy Shores

Coastal wetlands are secondary shorelines that are wet most of the time. These wetlands lie on the edge of the water, so they are flooded during high tides and remain wet even during low tides. Many coastal wetlands are estuaries. An **estuary** is a place where a river meets an ocean and freshwater mixes with salt water. Salt marshes, mangrove forests, and mud flats are three types of coastal wetlands.

Estuary

Coastal Changes

Hurricanes along the Gulf Coast of the United States have damaged or destroyed miles of coastal wetlands. These lands have been stripped of sediment or buried beneath it. Animals have been killed or left homeless. Plants have drowned or been buried under sand or mud. Because coastal wetlands provide a barrier between the open water and dry land, their disappearance also leaves coasts open to greater destruction by future storms.

Salt Marshes

Salt marshes are located where an ocean meets land. The amount of tidewater they receive depends on how sheltered they are from the ocean. Typically the tidal and wave action is gentle, so erosion is minimal. Plants that can tolerate submersion in salty water grow tall in these marshes. They provide shelter and food for the many animals that live there.

Mangrove Forests

Mangrove forests grow in tropical waters where a river flows into an ocean. The water here is brackish, meaning it's a mixture of salt water and freshwater. Mangrove trees are large trees with root systems that help them withstand the salty conditions and stay upright in the waves.

These roots take in oxygen from the air, restrict the amount of salt trees take in, and anchor the trees in the ground. They also collect sediment and provide a barrier between waves and the **mainland** shoreline, thus preventing erosion. A thriving mangrove forest is home to fish, crabs, shrimp, turtles, birds, and monkeys.

Mangrove roots

Mud Flats

Mud flats are sheltered coasts where slow-moving water deposits large amounts of sediment that build up into a flat area of mud. At high tide, the flat is covered with water. At low tide, the flat is exposed to the air. Because of the tidal changes, mud flats are also known as tidal flats.

The constant deposit of sediment makes the mud in mud flats very rich in nutrients. This supports the growth of **plankton**, which feeds animals such as snails, crabs, and oysters. Migratory birds rest on the flats, hoping to catch a bite to eat.

6

Barrier Islands and
Coral Reefs

Barrier islands and coral reefs are two types of shorelines with unique characteristics. Both of these shorelines support their own ecosystems and play a role in protecting other shorelines.

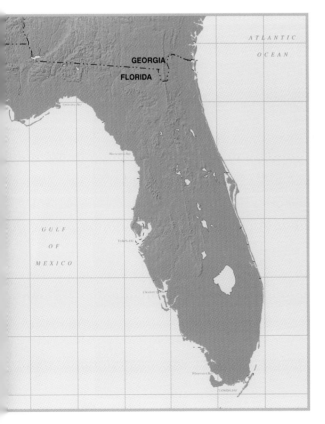

Barrier Islands

If you look at a map of the east coast of the United States, you'll see many little strips of land running parallel to the mainland. What are these tiny lands? They are barrier islands. A barrier island is an accumulation of sediment that occurs when longshore currents slow and drop sediment before reaching the coast. Over time, the sediment builds up into an island. The island then stands between the ocean and the mainland shore, separated by a body of water such as an estuary or **bay**.

Most barrier islands have a similar structure. The side facing the open ocean is a sandy beach. Sand dunes sit behind the beach. On the "back" of the island, coastal wetlands such as mud flats and salt marshes extend toward the mainland.

Barrier islands get their name from their ability to protect a mainland shoreline by forming a barrier between it and the ocean. Waves moving toward the shore

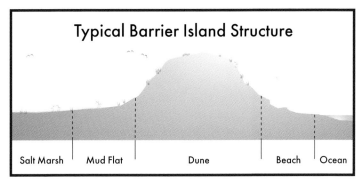

Typical Barrier Island Structure

Salt Marsh | Mud Flat | Dune | Beach | Ocean

hit the island instead of crashing full force into the mainland. Because they take the full hit, barrier islands undergo constant change from the water's erosive force.

Tracing the Path of Science

Hundreds of years ago, barrier islands were largely uninhabited and left to natural processes. Within the last decade, however, many barrier islands have been developed for communities and vacation resorts. To build houses, hotels, restaurants, and other structures, dunes are leveled and wetlands are filled in. This drastically changes the natural dynamics of the islands, harming both the shorelines and their plant and animal life. Today scientists focus their research on how to restore barrier islands to their natural state and preserve them for the future.

Green Island in Australia is a national park as well as a resort island. Its residents strive to balance tourism and the preservation of the land and water.

Coral Reefs

Coral reefs are reefs, or ridges, built from the skeletons of animals called *coral polyps*. Polyps live in colonies. When they die, they leave behind their hard outer skeletons. Over time, these skeletons fuse together, forming a reef. Many of these reefs rise above the surface of the water, creating a shoreline. Coral reefs that are close to a mainland form a protective barrier from erosion, much like barrier islands. Coral reefs also maintain their own ecosystems, providing food and shelter for at least one-fourth of all ocean species.

Great Barrier Reef

Coral reefs are sensitive to changes in their environment. They can grow only in warm, shallow ocean waters, and they need exposure to sunlight so the algae that live inside them can make food. In return, the algae provide oxygen and materials for the coral's skeletons. When the erosion of nearby shorelines increases the amount of sediment in the water, sunlight has a more difficult time getting through the cloudy water, reducing the amount of photosynthesis possible. If the algae die or leave the coral, the coral eventually die too.

Coral reefs also suffer when severe storms develop. Hurricane rains increase coastal erosion and deposition of sediment, limiting photosynthesis. Hurricane waves can smash reefs and break them apart. It can take years for a coral reef to recover from storm damage.

7

Saving Our

Shorelines

Many of the processes that shape the world's shorelines are natural, but others are caused by human intervention. Some human-made changes are made to protect land and people and restore beaches. Others are the result of human actions that have a negative effect on shorelines.

Technology Link

Scientists and government agencies need to monitor shoreline changes to identify potential problems and form plans to prevent or correct them. In the past, aerial photography was used to record coastal changes, but this was costly, inefficient, and didn't always provide clear, consistent results. So the United States Geological Survey developed SWASH (Surveying Wide-Area Shorelines) to track shoreline changes. SWASH devices are all-terrain vehicles capable of movement on land and water. Global Positioning Satellite (GPS) sensors are mounted on top of these vehicles, which roam shorelines taking measurements. Computers then combine the data into an overall "picture" of the beach that can be compared with past and future data.

Jetty

Jetties, Groins, and Seawalls

As more communities are developed along shorelines, erosion becomes a bigger threat to buildings, people, and beaches. Several structures have been designed to reduce shoreline erosion.

Jetties are long rock, concrete, or wooden structures built out into a body of water. Jetties are used to redirect the flow of water and sediment. They can help prevent erosion and open up waterways for boat passage.

Groins are structures similar to jetties that are used to reduce erosion on sandy beaches. Cities on barrier islands, for example, use groins as a defense against the waves. Groins run perpendicular across a beach and into the water.

Groins

Jetties and groins are effective at preventing erosion on the beach immediately behind them. However, since they stop sediment from moving down the coast, they prevent beaches farther down the coast from getting the sediment they need, thus speeding up erosion there. So while a jetty or groin may benefit one coastal community, it may damage another one down the coast.

Seawalls are defensive structures built on land along a shoreline. The walls are constructed parallel to the water to stop waves from crashing into communities on the coast. While they do keep communities safe, seawalls also encourage erosion in front of the wall because the strength of the waves deflecting off the wall carries away much, if not all, of the sediment in front of the wall.

A seawall in front of the city of Honfleur in France

Inquire and Investigate
Seawall Sediment

Question: How do seawalls affect sediment movement?

Answer the question: I think seawalls affect sediment movement by _____.

Form a hypothesis: Seawalls affect sediment movement by _____.

Test the hypothesis:
Materials
paint roller pan

2 cups of sand

piece of wood several inches
   high and at least 6 inches long

water

pitcher or watering can
   for pouring the water

Procedure
- Distribute the sand in the shallow end of the pan.
- Set the piece of wood (your seawall) on its long end across the sand so that most of the sand is behind it.
- Holding on to the wood, fill the deep part of the pan with water. Use your other hand to gently scoop the water forward to create small waves that push against your wall. Observe what happens to the sand on all sides of the wall.
- Increase the force of your "scooping" to make bigger waves. Observe what happens to the sand.

Observations: The sand directly in back of the wall doesn't move. The sand in front of the wall is washed away from the wall. The top layer of sand on the sides of the wall may begin to shift. Some may be pushed backward by incoming waves, and some may be carried forward by receding waves.

Conclusions: Seawalls affect sediment movement by eliminating or reducing the movement of sediment behind them and increasing the movement of sediment in front and to the sides of them.

Beach Nourishment

One method of beach restoration is called *beach nourishment*. Beach nourishment is the process of moving sand from another location onto an eroded beach. It can be used to "restock" a beach and/or make it wider.

Beach nourishment is an expensive project, but many cities whose beaches are vital to their economy find it worth the investment. Wider beaches also provide better protection against storms, and nourishment doesn't interfere with the flow of sediment like jetties, groins, and seawalls do. Unfortunately, beach nourishment can damage ecosystems. The dumping or pumping of sand can bury plants and animals and block sunlight that organisms need for photosynthesis. In addition, nourishment is a temporary solution because over time the new sand will be eroded like the old and will need to be replaced again.

Polluting Our Shorelines

Pollution is another source of change along shorelines. Trash left along the beach or dumped from boats and washed ashore can contain bacteria that are harmful to beachgoers and wildlife. Trash also poses a danger to animals that may be cut by it, become tangled in it, or eat it by mistake. Sewage, motor oil, pesticides, and other toxic materials that make their way into oceans introduce poisons and bacteria that may make beaches unsafe for people and animals swimming along the coast. Oil spills are particularly deadly to animals that make their home in the intertidal zones.

Scientist of Significance

Bostwick H. Ketchum (1912–1982) was a pioneer in the development of responsible shoreline management. He spent most of his career working for the Woods Hole Oceanographic Institution (WHOI), researching oceans and their health and productivity. From 1962 to 1977, he served as associate director of the institution.

Ketchum's early work focused on understanding oceans and their connection to the world's ecology. Later he devoted his time to studying the pollution and exploitation of coasts. He examined how human actions affect shorelines and proposed ways to monitor and correct problems. Ketchum's research was used to develop government policies addressing shoreline management.

Today, the BH Ketchum Award is given to an internationally recognized scientist who is a leader in shoreline research.

Air pollution may also contribute to shoreline changes. When fossil fuels are burned in cars and factories, they release heat-trapping gases, such as carbon dioxide, into the atmosphere. This has caused an increase in the temperature of the atmosphere known as global warming. Some scientists believe that continued global warming could eventually melt glaciers, causing sea levels to rise. Shorelines around the world would be redefined by these changes.

What can you do to help the Earth's shorelines? Pick up trash. Don't pour oil or toxic chemicals down drains or other places that might flow into open bodies of water. Plant trees to lower carbon dioxide levels in the air. Recycle garbage so it isn't burned. Taking steps to reduce land, water, and air pollution can preserve the world's shorelines.

Internet Connections for Changing Shorelines

http://www.mbgnet.net/salt/sandy/indexfr.htm
This student-friendly site provides information on the various types of shorelines as well as the tides and currents that change them.

http://www.onr.navy.mil/focus/ocean/habitats/beaches1.htm
Find out more about the types and characteristics of beaches and coasts from this Office of Naval Research site. It also includes information on how humans affect shorelines.

http://www.epa.gov/beaches/basicinfo.html
The Environmental Protection Agency presents information on beaches and what threatens them.

http://www.marietta.edu/~biol/biomes/shores.htm
Take a tour of sandy, rocky, and mangrove shores to experience the land and animals found along each of these shorelines.

http://www.nhptv.org/Natureworks/nwep6b.htm
Explore life in the zones along the shore. Learn more about how animals are adapted for life along changing shorelines.

Glossary

barrier island   (BAIR ee er EYE luhnd) long sandy island that runs parallel to a shoreline and protects the main shore from erosion

bay   (bay) area of sea enclosed by a wide inward-curving stretch of shoreline

beach drift   (beech drift) process by which waves move sand along a beach

cape   (kayp) narrow piece of land that juts out into water

current   (KER ent) flow of water in a particular direction

deposition   (dep uh ZISH uhn) deposit and accumulation of sediment by erosion

erosion   (uh ROH zhuhn) wearing away and movement of sediment by wind, water, or ice

estuary   (ES choo wair ee) area where a river meets an ocean and freshwater mixes with salt water

fault   (fawlt) break in the Earth's crust due to stress

longshore current   (LAWNG shor KER ent) current that moves parallel to a shoreline

mainland   (MAYN land) large landmass near an island or other smaller landform

photosynthesis   (foh toh SIN thuh sis) process by which plants and organisms such as algae use sunlight and carbon dioxide to make food

plankton   (PLANK tuhn) tiny organism that floats in a body of water

sand dune   (sand doon) mound of sand that accumulates at the back of a beach due to wind erosion

sandbar	(SAND bar) ridge of sand that accumulates when sand is deposited by a current
sediment	(SED uh ment) small particles of sand, soil, or rock
tectonic plate	(tek TAHN ik playt) piece of the Earth's crust
tide	(teyed) rise and fall of ocean water due largely to the gravitational pull of the Moon
wave	(wayv) series of ripples moving across the surface of the ocean

Index